LESSONS FROM THE
OBAMA 2012
GRASSROOTS CAMPAIGN

LESSONS FROM THE
OBAMA 2012
GRASSROOTS CAMPAIGN

What Two Devoted Volunteers Learned

AL KRAUSE / RUTH HIGGINS

iUniverse, Inc.
Bloomington

Lessons from the Obama 2012 Grassroots Campaign
What Two Devoted Volunteers Learned

iUniverse books may be ordered through booksellers or by contacting:

iUniverse
1663 Liberty Drive
Bloomington, IN 47403
www.iuniverse.com
1-800-Authors (1-800-288-4677)

Because of the dynamic nature of the Internet, any web addresses or links contained in this book may have changed since publication and may no longer be valid. The views expressed in this work are solely those of the authors and do not necessarily reflect the views of the publisher, and the publisher hereby disclaims any responsibility for them.

ISBN: 978-1-4759-5988-8 (sc)
ISBN: 978-1-4759-5989-5 (ebk)

Library of Congress Control Number: 2012920809

Printed in the United States of America

iUniverse rev. date: 11/13/2012

CONTENTS

Democracy is not a vicarious experience.
Bill Bradley on Charlie Rose, May 8, 2012

AUTHORS' NOTES

Without detailed notes for the first several months of our association with OFA, and with no intention of writing a book, we may have made some errors in exact times, places or sequence of events. However, we have made every effort to be as accurate and precise as our fallible memories allow.

We have named only paid staff and public figures; we have used pseudonyms or position titles for volunteers.

PREFACE

Physically, this is a small book, appropriate to the nature of the material. Our story is about the experience of two people—only that. We leave it to investigative journalists and political science professors to determine if our experience is typical of others who volunteered for Organizing for America (OFA), the Obama grassroots campaign.

People we didn't know directed most of our activity. When our cohorts questioned directions, we often said, "We're just cogs in the system, and we need to trust the organization."

Although our experience ended bitterly with accusations of poor communication and abuse of volunteers, this is also about great satisfaction in organizing a team that—for a time—was recognized as one of the strongest in the nation. In that process, we met many people whom we would never have met otherwise. We expect many of these people will be our friends for the remainder of our lives.

We remain passionately committed to the belief that Barack Obama is the right leader for America, and we continue to work to reelect him. Moreover, we persevere in holding out hope for the promise of "Organizing for . . ." as a movement that could reinvigorate progressive politics beyond this presidential election. To that end, we worked in our community to support a national congressional candidate, a state gubernatorial candidate, and state legislative candidates in this election. This effort could build networks that would support other local candidates and campaigns—school and park levies, for example—in the future.

We wrote this book for

- other campaign volunteers who could compare their experiences with ours and have their guards up in future campaigns;
- political science students planning to be campaign organizers who want to build strong morale for cohesive and vibrant volunteer groups; and
- leaders of organizations—particularly nonprofits—who want to recruit and retain quality people.

Al Krause and Ruth Higgins
October 2012

INTRODUCTION

In April, Al mailed the following letter to the widow of his only first cousin. She is a very conservative Republican:

Dear Cousin, We are very much involved in Organizing for America, the Obama grassroots campaign. Ruth was first recruited in July, and since then, we have been making calls in phone banks twice every week.

. . . The objective is to enlist volunteers. We make clear that we are not asking for money. Chicago does that.

Few people want to make calls. We enjoy calling. In two hours—from six to eight o'clock—we each make about sixty calls. The vast majority are NH for "not home." We hang up after four rings, and we don't leave messages. Many numbers are NLIS, "no longer in service." Some have moved; however, we suspect that more and more are dropping landlines for cells. (If you have an enterprising grandchild, she could become wealthy by figuring out how to produce white pages that include cell numbers.)

For most of the past six months, we have been calling people who headquarters in Chicago thinks are D[emocrats]. In a page of fourteen names, we typically have three conversations, maybe a dozen in an evening. Sometimes when we say, "I am a volunteer working on the Obama campaign," we hear hesitation, and we add, "I am working from a list that indicates you are an Obama supporter." The answer one evening was, "Never was and never will be." That fellow was friendly, as are most. Some Obama supporters thank us for our efforts.

When we find a person who is willing to volunteer we schedule a one on one, a face-to-face interview that tests potential volunteers who sign "I'm In" cards. [Name, address, phone number(s), email and a declaration, "I want to volunteer." The information is transmitted electronically to headquarters, which does not bode well for the post office workers' union that is spending money to advertise how necessary the postal service is.]

Al says that not since the army has he toed the line. He says he is a "cog" in the machine. Ruth is a "spoke." Her title is "Neighborhood Team Leader." Her neighborhood is the small towns and rural areas of our county, virtually all except Bellingham, the county seat. Total population of

Ruth's neighborhood is about sixty thousand people who are spread over some three hundred square miles. The "wheels" are the paid regional directors. We have had only four in Washington, but we are getting a few more.

Our wheel is Amie, a former sergeant in Army Intelligence who served in Iraq two times. She is twenty-seven, and her territory is five counties north of Seattle. Ruth is Amie's star. In February, Amie reported that Ruth's neighborhood with sixty members was ninth in the country in attracting volunteers . . . .

Cousin wrote back that she couldn't understand how "two apparently intelligent people can be so misguided."

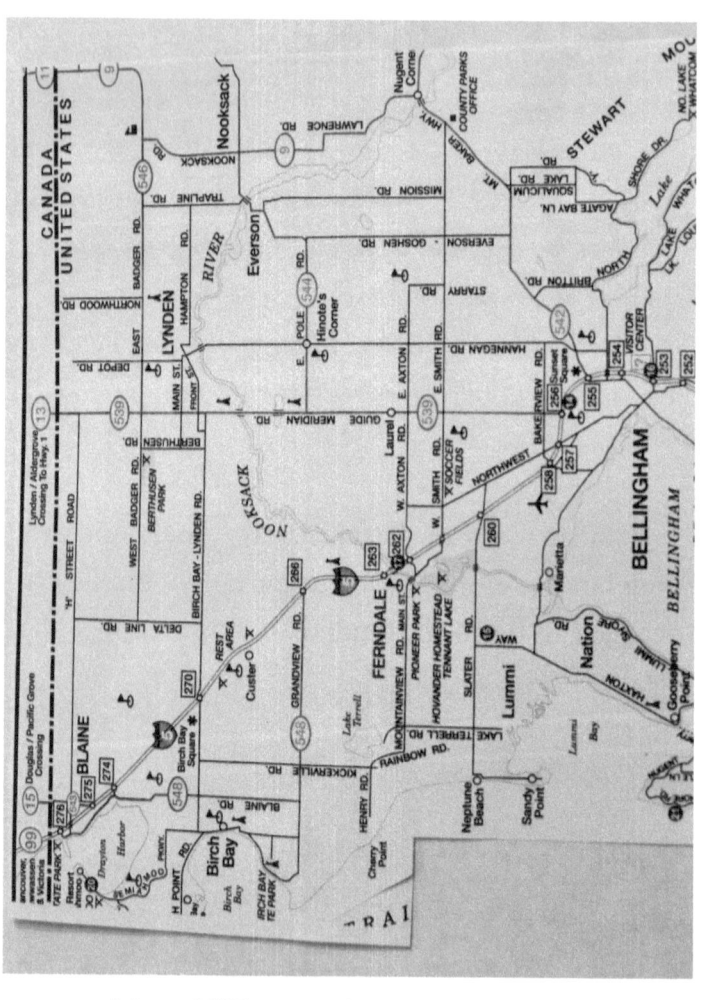

Map of Whatcom County, Washington,
provided by Bellingham Whatcom County Tourism,
www.bellingham.org

xviii

THE BEGINNING OF THE NORTHWEST WHATCOM NEIGHBORHOOD TEAM

Our involvement with Organizing for America (OFA) started in July 2011 when Ruth received a phone call from a resident of Bellingham's Leopold Retirement Residence, according to the caller ID. When asked if she would volunteer for a couple hours a week making phone calls from home for the president, Ruth agreed.

The next call was from a summer fellow,[1] suggesting that Ruth meet to talk about OFA, the president's grassroots campaign for reelection. On the appointed day, July 19, Ruth arrived at the appointed grill ten minutes ahead of the appointed time, sat right in front of the entrance door with a cup of tea, and waited. After about twenty minutes, Ruth took a circuit around the restaurant but saw no one who looked like her

---

[1] A seasonally selected intern working for the campaign.

intended date. After waiting another fifteen minutes, Ruth departed.

Within a very few days, the summer fellow called, and they discovered they each had waited for the other without making the connection. The fellow set up a virtual phone bank through VoteBuilder, the Democratic National Committee's and the Washington State Democrats' database. She outlined how Ruth could call people two hours a week to invite them to become active in the campaign. Ruth never did meet her.

Then Amie, the northwest regional field director, called and redefined the calling requirement as thirty-five calls a week and invited Ruth to meet one on one at the Bay Café to discuss OFA.[2] Vital, engaged, and enthusiastic, Amie asked if we could host an exploratory house party.

At the September 19 house party in our cottage, the Northwest Whatcom Neighborhood Team was born. Amie fielded many questions and concerns of the ten or so potential members

---

[2] Ruth would know her by the bobblehead doll of President Obama on the table.

present and we scheduled our first phone bank for September 27 at our cottage.

In October, the phone bank became a weekly event, every Tuesday, at various members' homes. Our mission on those calls was to grow the team, accomplished by inviting people to meet one on one with Amie. She and a volunteer campus organizer working with her came to Tuesday lunch at our place, followed by lessons for Ruth on how the various systems worked. Over the next several weeks, those one on one meetings transferred to Ruth and other team members.

During that time, individuals identified the roles they were interested in holding as core team members, including phone bank, data input, event, social media, and voter registration coordinators. Al chose the canvassing coordinator position.

The Northwest Whatcom Neighborhood Team was well on its way to becoming fully functional.

FALLING IN LOVE WITH AMIE

In this development period, Amie became like family for us. She drove her big, strong car fast up I-5 from her home in Redmond on the eastern side of Lake Washington. Usually she crossed the lake to Seattle to pick up her helper, who needed transportation to Bellingham for his job of organizing the Western Washington University campus. She seemed to enjoy all this time in her car. She joked that it was larger than the apartment she shared with her fiancé.

Amie and Nick met in Georgia at an army base and had been together three years, looking forward to being married after the election. Amie, who came out a sergeant, went to Iraq for two tours. She worked in counterintelligence in the Kurdish part of the country. Her mission was to protect U.S. information from theft. Nick was an intelligence analyst in Afghanistan.

Amie enlisted when she ran out of tuition money after two years of college. While she was in the service, her mother wrote to her about Candidate Obama. Amie became an enthusiastic supporter when GI benefits were strengthened, enabling her to complete college. She wrote her senior thesis on how Washington congressional candidates used "dog whistles" in their campaigns. With two more years of eligibility left, Amie talked about earning a doctorate, specializing in radical groups, to become a college professor.

The summer after college graduation, she volunteered with OFA. Shortly after, she was hired to lead five counties north of Seattle. Ruth was her first one on one. Her traveling partner stayed a volunteer. Having been an intern in

Maria Cantwell's Washington office in 2010, he was a tremendous source of information on politicians and their positions.

With full body and sweet face, wearing uniforms of tight sweaters and worn jeans, Amie struck us as genuine and a girl next door who, in many ways, was still a girl. But behind the femininity, we came to realize she was a tough soldier who was comfortable following orders from above. As we got to know Amie, we recognized that she could be manipulative. When we were doing right by her, we got smiles and hugs. When she was not pleased, she withheld those.

THRIVING ON PARTIES

OFA encouraged parties. We had some good ones that got Northwest Whatcom going. Everyone brought a dish or a bottle. We ate and drank well. Most memorable was our Halloween party. People were encouraged to come as "what do you want to be when you grow up." Ruth went all out with a long, black wig, cutwork consignment store black dress, sturdy black shoes, and sensible black stockings, topped off with black crystal-rimmed glasses. This was her idea of how an eccentric author looked. The book she carried was *You Can Write a Mystery*.

In San Francisco, we had both participated in improvisation workshops, and Ruth was particularly good at taking on a different personality.

Most of people who came to this party were new to OFA. Ruth didn't know them, and they didn't know her.

Sometime later, Ruth held a one on one meeting with a couple who had attended the party. They failed to recognize the confident, white-haired woman who greeted them at the café. Their recollection was of this weird thing in black, standing as if she were lost.

Accomplishing the real purpose of these parties, some of those strangers became our team's strongest members.

OBAMA AT THE PARAMOUNT

Amie invited us to help when the president came to Seattle in September. We were special. No one else from our team was invited.

Although Ruth had lived in Seattle in her twenties and thirties (and we had met and later wed there), we hadn't spent much time in the city since moving to Birch Bay nine years ago. It is 120 miles away, and we find that most of what we want to do is available in nearby Bellingham or Vancouver, British Columbia, only an hour north.

When we do go to Seattle, we usually stay with the couple in whose home we met and married. However, this time, their house was going to be full so we arranged to stay with Affordable Travel Club (ATC)[3] members, whose floating home is on Lake Washington. The hosts were gracious,

---

[3]   A hospitality exchange club, www.
      affordabletravelclub.net

and the floating home community offered a unique view of the world.

When Amie visited us shortly before the speech, she was as excited as we were. Just for the occasion, she had invested in a suit and high heels.

We were to be at the reception area of the convention center at eight thirty in the morning. Liz[4] had trouble and took us to the wrong end of Pike Street. With a corrected address, she got us to the convention center by our deadline. Amie had about twenty-five of her minions lined up for instructions. We volunteered for greeting duty at the front door. That meant we would be on our feet all morning, yet not exposed to as much boredom as those sitting and waiting for people at the registration desk. The first people started trickling in at nine o'clock, and there were never more than two parties at once until after noon. Our question at the door boiled down to, "Balcony or main floor?" If the person didn't know which, we'd ask, "How much did you pay?" Those who paid $100 sat in the balcony;

---

[4]   Our GPS that we named for Elizabeth, the pawnshop clerk who sold it to us.

those who paid more—as much as $7,700—sat at tables on the main floor where they were served lunch.

As the morning wore on, more volunteers showed up and disappeared. We viewed them as freeloaders, without realizing they were going to work in the Paramount Theater, crawling around the balcony, putting volunteer cards on seats, and doing other mundane tasks.

Some of the people we greeted were dressed for a cocktail party, some for church. These people, we soon understood, were there to have photos taken with the president. At the registration desk, they received green wristbands, identifying their status.

The only notables we greeted were legendary Seattle Sonics coach Lenny Wilkins and Bill Russell, the storied center of the Boston Celtics. To Wilkins, Al said, "Hello, Coach," and clutched his hand. Al didn't recognize Russell until his daughter said, "My father is here to introduce the president." Lenny smiled broadly. Bill was gaunt and frail but sporting a sharp suit.

Finally, about one o'clock, the doors were locked, and we were marched over to the Paramount Theater. Outside our windows, we had seen some demonstrators protesting about Jason Puracal, an American citizen unfairly jailed as an alleged drug dealer in Columbia who "Obama could set free."[5]

However, we weren't prepared for the throng of demonstrators at the corner as we turned toward the Paramount, representing many causes with bullhorns and chants. Security going into the theater was much easier than at an airport. This security was only checking our physical presence. We had been thoroughly vetted earlier.

The hardest part was watching waiters taking food into the floor tables. We had nothing except water from fountains. Al wanted to go home.

"We watch him on TV all the time," he said.

---

[5]   While writing this story, charges against Puracal were vacated, and he was set free.

Ruth prevailed.

After a short delay, we pink-tagged volunteers followed a guide to reserved seats about two-thirds of the way up the balcony. We hadn't contemplated how many people would be there. The theater, with twenty-eight hundred seats, was packed. We found two empty seats above a gang of students from Aviation High School with "Skunk Works 83" on the back of their shirts.

Then it was sit and wait. The president had been two hours late leaving Andrews Air Force Base and was now in Medina, having brunch with thirty-six people in the home of a retired Microsoft executive. They had paid $35,000 per couple.

A rock band came out and played some noise. Then came our leader, Amie, wearing her new suit and walking gingerly in her suede heels not yet broken in. And her hair was down. She told of serving in Iraq—to cheers from the crowd—when her mother wrote about this new guy running for president. Amie said she was able to complete college with the GI Bill that Obama had expanded.

Later, Amie told us she had trouble from the Secret Service prior to her speech. She argued that she had top-secret clearance in Iraq. However, they told her she couldn't touch the podium, something about the perils of anthrax. So there was Amie, standing back from the podium with the trembling pages of the speech she was trying to read. She said she was spooked when she glanced over at the teleprompter and saw it scrolling the Gettysburg Address as an equipment test.

After Amie, there was more delay. Then came Governor Christine Gregoire, who made a rousing speech arguing for the jobs bill. (Is she running for a job in the next administration?) There was more delay. We could see people backstage in line for pictures. The crowd got restless and started to chant.

Finally, Lenny and Bill appeared on stage, taking turns reading the speech they had received back at the convention center. Lenny was vibrant; Bill spoke softly.

At last, there he was, looking small beside the six-foot-ten Russell. We would never have grasped the excitement of an Obama speech from merely watching him on television. He played the crowd like an instrument. *Pianissimo* passages followed by *fortissimo* riffs produced a crescendo of roars from the crowd.

This was a partisan stump speech, a preview of what the Republicans could expect over the next year. No wonder New Jersey's Governor Christie, who had just announced he would not be a candidate, recognized how difficult running against Obama would be. We watched to see who jumped to their feet first as he ticked off accomplishment after accomplishment of his administration. The Skunk Works kids were first on their feet when he mentioned repeal of "Don't Ask, Don't Tell." And most of them surely weren't gay.

On the way back to the car, we realized we were no longer hungry or thirsty. We drove to Arlington, two-thirds of the way home, before stopping to eat our first meal since an early breakfast.

ONE ON ONES IN
SKAGIT COUNTY

Amie was having trouble organizing in Skagit, the county immediately south of Whatcom. In November, she asked us to help with recruiting volunteers and conducting one on ones. The evening before the appointed day, our phone bank team and others called people in Skagit County to schedule willing volunteers.

On the appointed day, we drove down to Mount Vernon, the county seat. We met in the headquarters of the county Democratic Party for training. Ruth, Al, and two others from Bellingham met the trainers who represented three-quarters of the OFA state cadre: Dustin, the state leader; Jeremy, the southwest regional director; and Amie, the northwest regional director. This was our first and last training to be one on one interviewers.

Al, who didn't know Dustin very well, asked him to be his trainer. That turned out to be a very good choice. The interview form was a series of questions that included a list of interests and affinity groups.

Dustin said, "Figure out what is most important about this person and concentrate on that. For example, I'm obviously a gay man, so LGBT[6] marriage is what's important to me."[7]

He also congratulated Al on telling his story of how much he had enjoyed canvassing door-to-door for Obama in 2008. That gave Al the feeling that he was prepared to interview.

We had expected that we would have to split up for the interviews, but we didn't. We both set out for Anacortes, a harbor town. Commercial ships dock in the harbor, and ferries travel to Vancouver Island and other points. There are also two refineries. Like Whatcom County, Skagit has a vibrant economy.

Someone had told Amie that Johnny Picasso's, a combination ceramics workshop and coffeehouse, would be a good place to meet people. She had never been there, but Liz was confident she could find the address. Most of the

---

[6]   Lesbian, gay, bisexual, and transvestite.
[7]   In the spring, Dustin left OFA to work for the Washington United for Marriage campaign.

Anacortes business district is along a narrow road from the highway to the water, where there are ship repair, dry docks, and other marine-related enterprises. Near the end, we found Johnny's.

When we got there, a couple guys were having coffee, and in a window seat was a young woman reading. She stayed most of the day. The manager, perhaps Johnny himself, was perfectly okay about us making his place into our temporary office, but one of his customers did ask what we were doing and showed some interest in Obama but not enough to accept an "I'm In" card.

We put small Obama signs on the tables in front of us and sat there like little chicks waiting for our parents to bring worms. When our interviewees arrived, our objective was to organize a meeting at Ned's home. We knew the address but not Ned's last name.

Our subjects were a mixed bag. Two of the women, who came at different times, knew each other and independently said they might co-host a phone bank. But they weren't interested in making calls. Al's best prospects were a couple who had been teachers in the local area and then went to Indonesia and from there to

Eastern Europe. She wrote a book about their experiences in tracing the history of a hero of Indonesia's independence. Her husband went to their car and brought Al a copy of her book that she autographed. The woman explained that she developed the material as a member of a writers' group in Anacortes. The members encouraged her to publish. The book, although self-published, looked professional.

Another of Al's prospects had worked for a landscaping firm. He was obviously well read and politically astute. One of his landscaping jobs was at a large waterfront estate owned by people in Seattle who wanted a caretaker. He had volunteered for the job, and he was enjoying the benefits there. He was an active tennis player and came to the meeting in shorts and a polo shirt. But he didn't like to drive at night, and he was uncomfortable about inviting people to a phone bank in his patron's home.

We were at Johnny's about six hours. Toward the end, Al ran out of prospects so he went for a long walk around the town, finding a good number of restaurants and cafés in this prosperous, blue-collar community.

We do know that the teaching couple became active members, meeting regularly with Ned (and presumably others) at his place. Ned became the neighborhood team leader.

TRAINING

During the year, we attended a few conventions that were really training workshops. For one, early on, volunteers from throughout the state gathered in the Machinists Hall in South Seattle.

The most memorable one, limited to Amie's five counties, was held in the Union Temple in Everett. Amie's performance was sharp and skilled. For most of the day, she was on stage,

varying the program with some talking alone and some use of PowerPoint presentations. Late in the afternoon, she performed a short skit involving other people to maintain attention.

That day, we met Chelsea, the new head of OFA Washington. Actually, she was the returning head, having led the Obama campaign in the state in 2008. If Hollywood were to make a movie about OFA, the director couldn't find a better star than Chelsea. Having made several stops at regional meetings that day, she seemed a little tired, but when she started to talk, she was relaxed.

After her talk, Al told her that, twenty years or so before, he had trained with the developers of the Interactive Method who wrote a book, *How to Make Meetings Work*. He said that since that time, he had not seen anyone engage an audience as well as she did.

It may have been at that meeting that we heard about the Snowflake structure. It showed how the campaign expected direction to flow down from the top to the neighborhood team leaders, then to the coordinators of various functions, and finally to the volunteer ranks.

Ruth, an experienced manager, adopted that system, believing what Kathy Paauw, a certified personal and professional coach says, "The most fundamental of all management skills is delegation—getting things done through others."[8]

---

[8]   "Paauwerfully Organized: Decluttering Schedules—spaces—minds," *Paauwer Tools Ezine* (May 2002), www.orgcoach.net/newsletter/May2002.html.

SNOWFLAKE ORGANIZATION

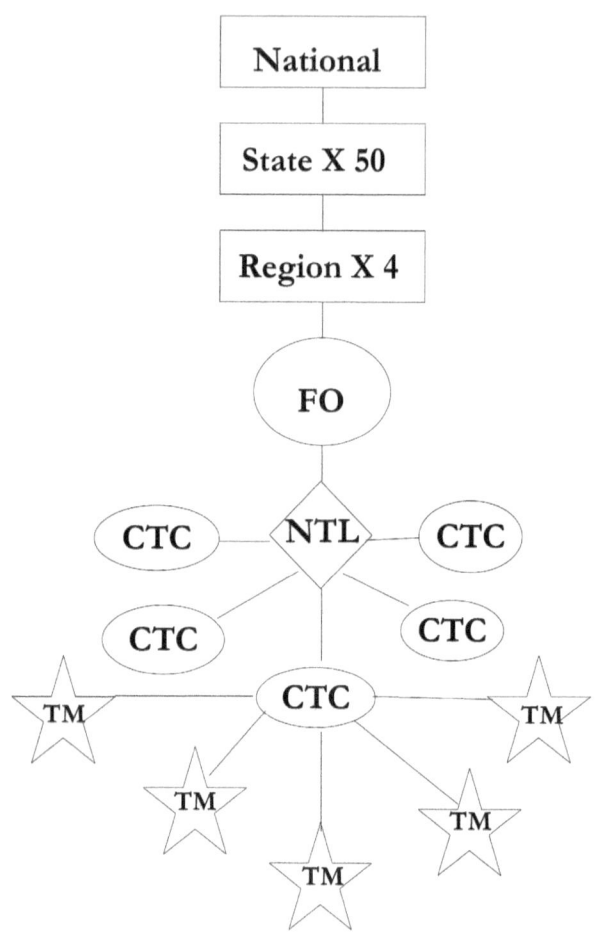

LEGEND:
FO = Field Organizer
NTL = Neighborhood Team Leader
CTC = Core Team Coordinator
TM = Team Member

Illustration by Ruth Higgins

TENSION BETWEEN
COUNTY DEMS AND STATE OFA

Ruth found that many of the strongest volunteer recruits were also active in the Whatcom County Democratic Party. Amie made it clear that we were working to reelect the president and Senator Maria Cantwell, who did not expect to have strong competition in Washington. We were to help elect Jay Inslee, the gubernatorial candidate. The Whatcom Dems were involved in every Democratic race in the county, plus the above.

Several times, Amie emphasized that the gubernatorial contest made Washington a battleground state. Obama winning a high percentage would lift Inslee to victory. She discouraged us from getting involved with the county Dems. It appeared to us that Amie was not paying attention to the county chair, Natalie McClendon, although she said she was coordinating by letting Natalie know what she was doing with an occasional phone call.

Despite never having been active with the county Democrats, we decided to accept the invitation to their holiday party.

When Natalie greeted us, we didn't expect she would know our names so we introduced ourselves as "working with Amie." Natalie looked puzzled and said she did not know Amie well.

We sat at a mostly vacant table, opposite a pleasant man who turned out to be a professional photographer and Natalie's husband. When she finished conducting the formal part of the program, Natalie joined him at our table, which led to lively conversation. We went home pleased that we had started a friendship with this attractive couple.

At our next visit from Amie, she said she would visit in person with Natalie. We mentioned our conversation with the 2008 Obama organizer with whom we thought Amie might want to connect because he was an active politician in our neighborhood. But Amie had no reaction. It was like, "He's not on our team now so he's of no account."

Increasingly, key members of our team asked, "Why can't we be in this campaign all together?"

One evening, when Ruth was at a phone bank and Al was at home, a woman from the Whatcom Dems called for Ruth. She wanted to know why OFA was not cooperating with the county organization.

In several conversations, when we raised this question with Amie, she dismissed the issue with, "They don't like us."

Another source of conflict in our team was the First Congressional District primary election. Washington would have an additional congressional seat in the next House of Representatives. A bipartisan commission, headed by a former governor, created the new district from the eastern side of King County, the state's largest, extending to the Canadian border and including our neighborhood. The Republicans put forth one candidate who had run unsuccessfully twice before. Five Democrats filed for the primary. Most members of our team had a favorite. Amie cautioned us not to choose until after the primary when the campaign would support the winning candidate.

In a very tough primary battle, Suzan DelBene—a former Microsoft marketing manager married to a Microsoft division president, who put a lot of money into her campaign—won. The Whatcom Dems endorsed someone else.

Meanwhile, in the same primary, at the last hour, Natalie and Matt Krogh, a popular environmentalist who we knew from previous water quality activism, filed for the state legislature against two very conservative incumbents. People in Whatcom OFA naturally wanted to work for "Nat and Matt," but we were discouraged from getting involved.

It appeared to us that Dwight Pelz, the Democratic state chair, was comfortable with this tension.

Along the way, we learned that OFA, with an increasing number of field organizers and interns, got its financial support from three campaigns: Obama's, Cantwell's and Inslee's. DelBene's campaign, with lots of money, joined after the primary.

Later, when Ruth was making OFA calls from home as a virtual phone banker, we noted that the script ended with:

> *Thanks! I wanted to let you know that this call was paid for by Organizing for America-WA, a project of the Washington State Democrats, and not authorized by any candidate or candidate committee.*

The purpose of those calls volunteer recruitment for specific upcoming events related to our candidates' campaigns.

As we were completing this manuscript, we called OFA state headquarters in Seattle. The receptionist answered with, "Organizing for America, the Obama Campaign."

Reader, you figure!

EVER-INCREASING NEED TO RECRUIT VOLUNTEERS

On the last day of June, Ruth's volunteer roster listed sixty-five names, with about one-third expressing an interest in phone calling. The prior Thursday evening, we had only three callers plus one data inputter, not a very good turnout from a pool of a possible twenty-two people who had said they were interested in making calls. Despite our small team, we called 167 numbers with fifty-five conversations.

Some of our volunteers said they didn't like to make phone calls because they and people they knew were tired of getting phone calls at their own homes. Some callers were slaves to their scripts despite the advice they should use their own words. They were just not comfortable doing that.

The best callers sit down and start dialing. But many come with baggage. For example, one woman was always talking about what she anticipated the people she called would say, based on her hearing the news, mostly cable TV and talk radio.

Another volunteer came to a phone bank and spent most of the evening lobbying another volunteer, a member of the local planning commission. The nag kept talking about something he wanted from the planning commission, but his issue turned out to be under a different office. The nagger never came to another phone bank. However, he later did spend two hours on two successive days canvassing door to door. And he never came back to canvass again.

A minor hazard of phone calling is the possibility of nasty responses. "Fark off" or "Go fark yourself" are uncommon but memorable. Al argues that, for every nasty response, you will have many, say ten, which will be friendly. In some cases, even if they don't volunteer, callees will express appreciation of our work for Obama.

Not all volunteers come from phone calls. One day when Ruth was meeting with Colleen and a summer fellow in the café at the local Haggen store, the man in the booth behind Ruth said, "Nice shirt." She was wearing the campaign

T-shirt with the image of the president over "Made in America" on the front and a replica of his birth certificate on the back. She had a recruit.

We held phone banks twice a week for several months, with limited attendance at each. When one of the phone bank coordinators had to resign because of work demands, we consolidated his Tuesday session with the Thursday one, in hopes of increasing the attendance. That did not happen.

We continue to believe that phone calls are the seeds that grow the team, the fuel that runs the engine.

A PARTICULARLY GOOD
PHONE BANK

On July 5, in addition to Independence Day, television news was celebrating the TomKat divorce, George Zimmerman's million-dollar bail, and Casey Anthony's phone interview with CNN's Piers Morgan. But there was very little attention to confirmation of the Higgs Boson, arguably the most significant scientific development thus far in the twenty-first century.

We were not in the mood for the evening's phone bank, which had been moved to our cottage because the scheduled host asked for a trade. The confirmer only reported the people who weren't coming, so we faced each other with the possibility that we would be the only callers.

Then Russ arrived. He was the one who "self-recruited" in the Haggen café and he had come to the previous four phone banks, twice a week. Russ is a guitarist and singer. His smooth friendly voice and knowledgeable enthusiasm for the president make him an excellent caller. In addition to being an efficient caller and better-than-average recruiter, Russ introduced an addition to our list of hard asks. When a callee expressed support but pleaded being too busy to volunteer, Russ would suggest he or she talk up Obama and Democratic values among family, friends, and coworkers.

"Word of mouth is valuable," he explained.

We made this standard in our routine.

Shortly after Russ, Molly arrived. With white hair and a lean body, it was difficult to judge Molly's age. Along with diced watermelon, Molly brought enthusiasm that kept the group upbeat. She didn't have spare minutes on her cell phone plan, so she used the one remaining cell phone the campaign provided. We started with three campaign phones. One died, and Amie recalled one.

Our data input coordinator came, followed by two data trainees, a husband-and-wife team. The husband brought his slim Apple laptop that couldn't find our WiFi, so he moved to our studio to use a desktop computer. With his wife reading information off the call sheets, halfway through the evening, the coordinator proclaimed the new team successful.

At six thirty, a woman who Ruth had recently interviewed called, saying she had visitors who had just left. Was it too late for her to come?

"Never too late. We'd be thrilled to see you," Ruth said.

Marie arrived before seven o'clock, sat down, and called diligently, completing four pages before we stopped at eight o'clock. We had a full cottage and a successful phone bank with 267 calls and forty-two conversations.

As people packed up, Al reported his best call in memory. Looking down his final call sheet, he spotted a difficult-to-pronounce name that he thought might be Sikh or Muslim, a twenty-nine-year-old female. An older woman's voice answered the phone.

"Yes, my daughter is here."

Coming to the phone, the young woman said she was an Obama supporter, but she was a college student, going away this coming weekend, and could not volunteer.

After mentioning that volunteers would be needed until November, Al said, "I think I may know you. Did you graduate from Blaine High School?"

"Yes."

"And after your dad died, did you cover your head?"

"Yes."

"Did you work at BP?"[9]

Now laughing, she said, "Yes."

---

[9]   The British Petroleum refinery near us.

"Were you at a benefit dinner for Somalia Relief at the ReSources meeting room?"

"Yes, I remember you and your wife."

"We've been thinking it would be good to invite the guy from Egypt who works at the Sharia mutual fund and his wife and you and your boyfriend out for a meal."

"We're married now. That would be nice."

"I recall vividly how great you looked in that outfit. There must be an appropriate Muslin name for it."

"I made it all myself. Thank you."
What a way to end the evening.

A YOUNG FIELD ORGANIZER STRUGGLES

Colleen was an ambitious volunteer who caught on with Amie. A recent graduate of Western Washington University who majored in political science and economics, she supported herself working at the Red Robin restaurant, a burger chain where Amie had also labored while attending college.

After several months serving as a spring fellow, Amie encouraged Colleen to become a paid field organizer. She turned down a position in Virginia and then Ohio, hoping to stay in her home state of Washington. Undefined circumstances appeared to slow down Colleen's promotion. However, by the beginning of May, when the new OFA office opened in Seattle, Colleen went on the payroll.

A tiger caller at phone banks, Colleen's effectiveness was questionable. She talked so fast that we wondered if people at the other end were able to understand her.

When one of our stalwart phone bank coordinators took a temporary assignment in Everson, he suggested we expand our team into eastern Whatcom County. With Amie's approval, we recruited volunteers and met at a Whatcom Educational Credit Union branch. About fifteen people attended our first meeting. No one wanted to take on the leadership role. We decided to continue phone banks while contacting other prospective candidates.

The original Wednesday meeting day didn't work for some people, so we tried a Monday date. That had even lower turnout. Colleen, as the newly appointed field organizer who would take over management of that team, came to her first East Whatcom meeting in late May. Draping herself over a chair, waving her hands, and talking fast, she did not seem to impress the group.

Several of these volunteers were experienced campaigners and active members of the Whatcom County Democrats. One couple organized a potluck supper for Cinco de Mayo, inviting a number of politically active members of the community. Although we met engaged and politically knowledgeable people, none signed up to volunteer. Despite what we had felt was great energy and eagerness to work for the cause, the reelection of President Obama, the fledging team soon disintegrated.

Apparently, East Whatcom members did not want to do phone banks, despite making five hundred calls with fifty-two conversations in April. People from the furthest east locales were tired of driving to Everson (a round trip of nearly fifty miles), the field organizer did not want to drive that far (almost forty miles from Bellingham), and cell phone service was slow and unreliable.

With little or no testing of different meeting days, voter registration, or canvassing possibilities, at some level the campaign decided it would not be a good use of resources to pursue a separate East Whatcom Team. It was folded into the Northwest Whatcom Team, which was renamed just "Whatcom" to represent the entire county, excluding the city of Bellingham.

The Glacier member, who took on a social media coordinator position, created one valuable remnant of that effort. He started the OFA East Whatcom County Neighborhood Team Facebook page, to which he posted at least daily, if not several times a day.

An effort to organize on Lummi Island followed a similar pattern. However, there we had a willing leader, but few volunteers. The population was sparse, and known Democrats were already committed to the party. Following a meeting with Colleen, the campaign severed that nascent team from the Whatcom Team and folded it into the Lummi Peninsula, an area that included the Lummi Nation and several other residential communities. That region became part of the North Bellingham Neighborhood Team.

Wanting Colleen to succeed, we suggested she study Krystal Ball, now part of *The Cycle* on MSNBC. There is enough of Colleen in Krystal's expressions that we thought this suggestion might be helpful. Krystal, who ran for Congress, is able to sit with minimum movement, talk slowly and distinctly, and modulate her voice to emphasize her points. We believed she would be a great role model for Colleen. We never heard if she ever watched Krystal on TV.

OPENING
NEW SEATTLE OFFICE

The draw was Debbie Wasserman Schultz, one of our top five favorite political television personalities.

Getting its own Seattle office was a big deal for Washington's OFA, as our leaders had shared office space with the state Democratic Party for several months. The new space was located south of the Seattle business district on the edge of Rainer Valley, crime central. When we made a wrong turn off the freeway, Liz safely got us back on track.

The building is in a mixed neighborhood with an attractive new condominium building and worn warehouses. Ours was one of the most worn. There were two entrances—one for press and Inslee contributors—and the other for the rest of us. The campus organizer who had been to our home several times with Amie greeted us and led us downstairs to OFA's office space.

It was a long, narrow room, where our leaders were working on laptops and smaller devices. When we mentioned that Natalie McClendon, the current chair of the Whatcom County Democrats, had announced for one of the 42nd Legislative District Representative seats, OFA State Director Chelsea turned from her iPad in surprise. Really!

On the way to the speakers' area, we ran into a cheerful, young woman, a Western Washington University graduate who had just learned that she had a job in development at University of Washington starting in the fall. This summer, she was interning for Inslee. She was a good friend of Colleen, our field organizer, and she said they talked by phone almost every evening.

The auditorium was a loading dock with a large roll-up door that would be the speaker's entrance. A platform of plywood stacked on packing boxes was high enough that all the people standing could see. A few front row chairs were reserved for the elderly and lame. Moving forward, we got close behind the chairs.

Congresswoman Schultz, head of the Democratic National Committee, looked smaller to us than we imagined from seeing her on television. During the preliminary speeches, we watched her interact with her aide. Out came a sheaf of papers that looked like a script. Debbie leafed through it and handed it back before going up on the plywood. She could talk fast into a riff, almost as well as Obama, and the audience roared crescendos of approval.

Dwight Pelz, the state party chair, also proved to be a dynamic speaker. Congressman Jim McDermott, Seattle's most popular progressive, introduced Jay Inslee, Washington's Democratic candidate for governor. McDermott's avuncular smile and crown of white hair made us feel that the drive down I-5 in the torrential downpour was worthwhile, but we cannot remember anything he said.

Inslee had been elected to Congress from two districts on either side of the Cascades. He is a big man, in contrast to the slight Rob McKenna, his opponent who is currently Washington's attorney general. At the outset, McKenna was favored in the August primary. Inslee gained more votes and his surprise showing generated optimism for the general election. We heard that Inslee attributed his tally to the efforts of OFA and called to express his appreciation.

That day in Seattle, Inslee was as dynamic and down to earth as Shultz—or the president. We drove home fired up, confident that Inslee was a good candidate.

OUR VERY BIG DAY

In February, we knew well in advance that President Obama was coming to the Seattle area. Then we learned he would be in Bellevue, the technology capital on the eastern side of Lake Washington. When Amie offered us the coveted opportunity to volunteer, we waved her off, saying that, having seen him last September, some of our leading team members deserved the opportunity. However, Amie said our people would be able to see the president when he spoke in the morning at the big Boeing plant in Everett.

She was adamant, telling us, "Leadership wants you there."

However, Amie told Ruth to nominate one outstanding volunteer to join us. Ruth selected the data input coordinator who efficiently and effectively trained, scheduled, and monitored a growing cadre of vital volunteers.

The president would be speaking at a luxury hotel in the middle of one of the most upscale downtowns in the country. All the Fifth Avenue brands were there. A Microsoft sign topped the tallest building. Having hustled down I-5 to be on time, we were so early that we were told to go out for coffee.

Returning to the hotel, we found security everywhere. A phalanx of Bellevue police cars lined the street, plainclothes men paced throughout the hotel, and a soldier in full battle gear strode up the side street. In the hall outside the restrooms, Al asked a detective if there were a special emergency.

"No," he said, "it's just routine."

Jeremy, Amie's counterpart for the southern part of the state, became our keeper. Four of us volunteers were on his team. Two went to the elevators from the parking garage to guide people to the registration tables. We were given "I'm In" cards to distribute to the people in line waiting to enter the hotel.

This was going to be a long day. The president was already in Everett. Like kids tracking Santa Claus, we learned he would again be going to Medina, the richest suburb on the eastern side, for brunch at the home of a cofounder of Costco. There again the contribution was $35,000 per couple. Our folks were getting a late lunch but at a discount. A couple could get a green wristband—meaning a picture—for only $5,000.

The people in this line were better dressed, better looking, and chattier than those we greeted in September. Few showed enthusiasm for the "I'm In" cards. Some said they were already getting messages from the campaign every day. We worked our way up and down the line that went around the hotel. We were in a party mood despite the damp chill. Around the corner, there was Big Bill Russell. Al grabbed his hand but didn't get a press. With him was his daughter, whom we had seen before, a tall woman maybe six-foot-five, and a modest-sized sidekick with dyed and coiffed brown hair to match his suit.

"That's Fred Brown," someone said.

"Who?"

"Downtown Freddy Brown, the captain of the Sonics championship team."

A campaign worker rescued Bill and his party from the line. A few minutes later, two young couples took their place.

Al said, "You're standing right where Bill Russell was!"

"Is he head of Russell Investments?" one of the women asked.[10]

When the line got short, Jeremy led us back inside the hotel. With the event registration tables and the campaign workers, there was little room in the small lobby for guests entering the hotel. Amie pulled us to one side. She had two green wristbands.

In a confidential voice, she said, "We got you in to meet the president."

Ruth's jaw dropped.

"And to have your picture taken," added Amie.

Ruth's jaw took another dip. Tears filled her eyes. She was speechless, a rare occurrence. We huddled together on a vacant couch in a state of shock.

"Can't be just us," said Ruth. "Probably a group picture with all the other volunteers."

When Amie came back to us, Al said, "This is going to be a group picture, isn't it?"

---

[10]   Russell Investments, recently moved from Tacoma to Seattle, is one of the nation's largest institutional investment firms.

We can't remember clearly, but we think Amie laughed as she sent us up the steep escalator. There on the ballroom level, Jeremy guided us through turns in the hall to reach a security check that was as easy as it had been at the Paramount.

Out of the security line, we were in a large space outside the ballroom with some other volunteers. We found green wristbands on none except a family of six, waiting patiently outside a curtained-off section.

There we saw Chelsea, the state OFA director. We credit her for choosing us for the photo, making for us what will surely be one of the great days of our lives.

Patricia, another of Amie's counterparts, was sitting at a table selling T-shirts and other campaign items. A television camera crew coming through security provided entertainment for a half hour. The Secret Service agents, with the help of a dog, inspected every item on a dolly.

We reunited with the data input coordinator, who had been doing security duty with a Secret Service agent. We peeked through the doorway to the ballroom to see people eating, which should have made us hungry, but we were too excited to care. We were told that food for volunteers was in a room down a hallway. We didn't bother.

Eventually, we—along with other volunteers—entered the ballroom and stood against the back wall, as instructed. A speaker, a bookstore owner, told how a stimulus loan enabled him to keep his small business open. A rock band played two very loud sets.

Our other entertainment was watching the Secret Service agents surrounding the stage. We counted nine of them. Each appeared to be watching a specific area without wavering. One agent was a young woman in a neat blue business suit. The rest were male. We figured a diagram mapping their viewing area guided their stoic gazes.

A line formed at an exit door on the left wall of the ballroom. After joining that queue, we noticed that all the people had green wristbands. We didn't recognize any other volunteers. The line snaked around tables where waiters were clearing the last of the dishes. Through the door, the line went halfway around a dimly lit room. Most of the people were enjoying the wait, smiling and laughing. Bill and Downtown were close behind us and the daughter remembered us. We told her a woman who took their place outside had asked if Bill were head of Russell Investments.

"Don't we wish," she laughed.

At the end of the line was a black curtain similar to the ones we had seen in the ballroom foyer. We could see flashes. Before we had time to think, we were through the curtain. A woman took Ruth's purse. The photographer stood there with a big lens and no tripod. We entered a bubble of warmth surrounding the president. His huge, warm hand enveloped Ruth's small cold one.

She said, "Hello! I'm your neighborhood team leader in Whatcom County, the most northwestern county in this northwest state."

With that wonderful smile and absolute focus, he said, "What you are doing is very important. Thank you very much."

Al has never been able to smile on command. Neither "cheese" nor anything else works. So he planned a joke. "We thought you would be cardboard," he said as we moved into position.

The president said, "No, I'm the real thing!"

He laughed and so did we. The camera flashed twice.

We were back in the ballroom against the wall when Bill and Lenny began their introduction. In the smaller room with a smaller crowd, the speech was not as exciting as at the Paramount. It did not matter to us.

CANVASSING TOGETHER

Sunday, the first day of July, was the start of our canvassing together. Al, after sitting out the Sunday before, was in the mood to be a good cog. Ruth spent much of the previous day matching the walking lists with maps that Colleen had provided from the database. It took Ruth about two hours to process each packet, only enough for a one- or two-person, two-hour shift.

Colleen, accompanied by an intern, came for training shortly before one o'clock. When we told her that the maps were difficult to follow, she said, "Well, they get you started in the right direction."

She gave us a handful of Inslee brochures, explaining that the names on our lists were of people identified as "sporadic voters." Our objective was to confirm that and convince them to vote for Obama, Cantwell, and Inslee.

That morning the *Seattle Times* editorial page endorsed Rob McKenna, Inslee's Republican opponent. The paper's reasoning was that McKenna, having been attorney general, was more aware of the state's problems. Particularly, they favored his positions on education and taxes. Neither Colleen nor her intern was aware of that recommendation.

We chose to work the turf nearest our home that included the housing development we had canvassed in 2008. While we could have walked directly to almost all of the locations from our home, they were each widely spread out. We took our car, even though we were concerned that starting and stopping would use a lot of gas.

Ruth went in to the first house. The folks there said they were not Democrats because of Obama's "socialism." One of our interviewees said yes for Obama, but he did not know Inslee. Al gave him a brochure. The man said he was for Cantwell. When asked if he intended to vote, he said, "Not likely because it doesn't make any difference."

We took turns driving, with the passenger going to the door. We never approached a house together. When two or three homes were close to each other, we both got out of the car to share the doors. For safety, we stepped back from the door after ringing the bell or knocking, making sure we had good footing should we need to make a hasty departure. With very few exceptions, we found people friendly, even when they were opposed to Obama. A few spoke crudely but rarely in a menacing way.

In two hours, we drove nine miles, even with Liz's help. We only got to eighteen doors for seven conversations. Three were strong for Obama and Cantwell, but none for Inslee. Others were undecided on one or another. Six said they would vote. One said maybe.

A fellow canvasser went to twenty-one doors in another area and found no one home.

Slim pickins!

In response to our complaints, Colleen later said she would get us lists that were more compact and within our own precinct. However, that expectation didn't materialize.

We received walking lists for Blaine that took two long evenings. Again, the homes were spread out. We frequently parked the car and went in different directions.

Colleen had told us the sporadic voters on our lists were expected to be on the fence this year. In our limited experience, our canvassees did not meet that definition. Some were solid Democrats; others were certain Republicans.

Sometimes people with different names lived at the addresses listed, not unexpected because people move between elections. At one large house, a man's name was listed with a different woman's name, also not unexpected because women often retain their former names. However, the attractive, professional-looking woman who answered the door was irritated when Al asked if she were the person with the feminine name. She had never heard of that woman. She and her husband had lived there for some time. She would have called him to testify if he had not been busy bathing their young children.

LAST DAYS OF AUGUST

Part One: Voter Registration

Our fateful last days began on August 9, two days after the primary election, when Ruth got an e-mail message from Colleen, addressed to her and two other female team leaders, saying,

> *Hi, Ladies, So I know that it is super last minute, but we need to do a voter registration drive this Saturday. So no canvassing at all[11] but just registration. Thankfully, we can get all of those people who did not go out canvassing registering voters. Haha. Let me know if you have questions or need help planning!*

Ruth shot back:

> *Received at 9:10 p.m. Thursday—Planning???? We'll see what we can do, but really?*

---

[11] We had no canvassing scheduled.

Ruth had a number of issues with this directive:

- The campaign had suspended voter registration in the month running up to the primary, with the vague understanding they would bring it back sometime after that election. There was nothing about four days later with two-day notice.
- The voter registration (VR) coordinator was new to her role, having replaced the previous one due to health issues. Putting such pressure on her at this stage of her development was not good management.
- The VR coordinator had committed to working a shift in the Whatcom Democrats' booth at the Northwest Washington Fair on that Saturday.

In telephone discussion with Colleen on Friday, Ruth said, "In my career, we talked a lot about just-in-time management. There are times when I call this not-quite-in-time direction."

Colleen and Ruth agreed that the Whatcom Team would combine with Bellingham on Saturday. Ruth passed that on to the VR coordinator and asked her to call half of the VR volunteers, with Ruth calling the other half, to let them know what was happening and to invite them to meet at eleven in the morning at the Bellingham OFA Office.

Ruth reported there on Saturday, took the Fairhaven beat, and got one registration. The VR coordinator later said that she arrived about eleven thirty in the morning and found no one in the office. Taking a clipboard and forms, she went to the farmer's market but saw no one she recognized there. She left town without obtaining any registrations. No other Whatcom team members turned up.

It was quite a time-wasting fiasco in Ruth's view.

Part Two: Core Team Meeting and Canvassing

In a meeting on Friday, August 17, Colleen asked Ruth to call a core team meeting as soon as possible. The purpose would be for Colleen to talk about stronger team building and to emphasize the importance of the hard ask—not taking no for an answer when recruiting volunteers.

Despite the fact that Ruth and the events coordinator had scheduled the core team meeting for Tuesday, August 28, as directed, an e-mail soon arrived from Colleen:

> *I would like to stop by and talk to everyone, but if there isn't*
> *a large turnout, it won't make sense to miss call time for it.*

Had she forgotten the purpose? Ruth reported that she expected sixteen people.

At the core team meeting, Nolan, a summer fellow, came in Colleen's place.[12]

We had an abundant potluck meal with the ten people who did show up, sitting around a large table with Nolan. These participants were some of the best workers and thinkers on the team. They peppered Nolan with questions and complaints. He was patient and did his best to explain for the campaign.

One of the members, who had been unaware of any friction, asked, "Why are you so angry?"

Al exclaimed, "Because we're being treated like f—king army privates."

He had been one. He knew how it felt.

After the meeting, Nolan stayed to explain how to create walk sheets for canvassing from VoteBuilder and demonstrated a new scheduling

---

[12] At three forty-five in the afternoon, Colleen had sent an e-mail advising that she had a migraine headache and was unable to drive, but Ruth did not read that before leaving home for the dinner.

feature for data inputting. He was looking like an angel until he said, "I've done my three months. I'm moving on next week."

Another subject of the August 17 meeting was the upcoming schedule. We were to continue with weekly phone banks for now with the possibility of doing two per week soon. We were to hold weekly voter registration and canvassing events, starting as soon as possible.

Al reactivated himself as canvassing coordinator[13] and wrote to the seventeen team members who had originally volunteered to canvass, asking for their participation on Sunday, August 26. During the week, he phoned each. Some were away or did not answer. None attended, but a new recruit came, bringing her fourteen-year-old daughter.

We chose a rural area and asked the new recruits to ride along with us for an introduction to the campaign and training purposes. They were enthusiastic workers who knocked on their share of the doors. However, the addresses were widespread, and we only opened twenty doors with fifteen conversations.

---

[13]   He had resigned in June.

When she heard our numbers, Colleen said the goal for Whatcom was eighty doors, without providing information on how this number had been determined. Amie was quick to send an email saying that four people canvassing together was wrong, without asking for or giving a reason.

On Saturday, August 25, Colleen wrote to Ruth:

> *I think we need to have a meeting to go over OFA roles. I understand you are coordinating with the 42 LD[14] candidates' campaigns. That is fine and something we should do; however, it is something I should be managing as the field organizer. Also, I want to make sure that we are on the same page in terms of events, CTMs,[15] and what we need to accomplish in Whatcom County to succeed. I know things change last minute at times, and it might seem like we do events for no reason. But they are all to expand our team building and to accomplish our goals. Let me know if there is a day next week that we can meet!*

Ruth's answer the same day included, in part:

---

[14]   Legislative district.
[15]   Core team members.

I welcome the opportunity to discuss OEA rules again, as some of the directives have been confusing and contradictory. I do try to stay on the same page as the campaign, running things by you to confirm before I act, like asking about carrying the campaign material of the legislature candidates when we canvass. I attended a meeting yesterday (at Whatcom Dems office) in my role as a future PCO, and the subject of coordinated canvassing came up. As I mentioned the last time we met, I think written procedures or guidelines would minimize some of the confusion and contradictions, as well as promoting consistent activity that can be replicated downline.

Part Three: Democratic Convention Watch Party

In that same August 17 meeting, Colleen said that, in addition to scheduling the core team meeting, Ruth should plan for a Watch Party to view President Obama's acceptance speech at the Democratic National Convention on September 6. Ruth immediately sent out a cancellation notice for the scheduled phone bank and contacted the events coordinator. They contemplated having to find a location for up to forty people, based on the experience of the January State of the Union speech-watch.

At another meeting on August 22, with two other neighborhood team leaders, a summer fellow, and newly recruited fall fellow (promised to the Whatcom team), Colleen said the September 6 event should have a short phone bank prior to the convention watch party.

Ruth protested that was a bait-and-switch tactic, as the criteria for phone bank locations differed from that for parties. She had delegated the assignment to her events coordinator, as in the Snowflake, the organizational structure taught at an early training session.

Colleen replied, "That didn't work. We don't use it anymore."

This was news to Ruth.

After debating back and forth in e-mails and by phone about who said what when, Ruth followed with this e-mail:

> *I do not want to get into a pissing contest with you, but I came away from our 8/17 meeting with the distinct understanding that this was to be a Democratic Convention Watch Party with volunteer recruitment like the SOTU*[16] *one, as I noted at the*

---

[16] State of the Union.

*time, and immediately sent out the message below.[17] At our 8/22
meeting, you informed us that we should have a short phone
bank prior to the watch party. Today, 8/27, you are describing
it as a phone bank interrupted by watching the convention. That
fits my description of a changing definition. Communication is a
function of transmission and reception, often distorted by noise.
We may both benefit from reducing that noise.*

Ruth then sent out an e-mail to all concerned,
"Cancel the Cancellation of 9/6 Phone Bank," after
confirming that the host could reschedule. Despite
a very complex and crowded calendar, he assured
Ruth he would be at home on that evening.

The next morning, Amie called, chastising
Ruth for disrespecting Colleen, saying, "She's the
best field organizer in the state."

Ruth responded, "Really? Would you prefer
for me to call her a liar?"

The next morning, as Ruth prepared for her
meeting that afternoon with Colleen, Al wrote
this memo for Ruth:

---

[17] Announcing the 9/6 phone bank was being canceled
in favor of a watch party.

Dear Ruth, Concerned about how Colleen spoke to you Monday. I went to the bible for organizers, Rules for Radicals, by Saul Alinsky.[18] *He started his chapter on Communication with:*

> *One can lack any of the qualities of an organizer—with one exception—and still be effective and successful. That exception is the art of communication. It does not know what you know about anything if you cannot communicate it to your people. In that event, you are not a failure. You are just not there. Communication with others takes place when they understand what you are trying to get across to them.*

In reviewing past correspondence, I found an e-mail of August 20 from Jeremy Bird, the Chicago OFA boss, addressed to me on our KrauseHiggins user name, which neither of us used for OFA communications. The e-mail asked me to host a convention party in Blaine for the president's address at the convention. There was no mention of a phone bank and no reference to OFA Whatcom. Moreover, his words are mostly cheerleading, without meaningful discussion of party strategy. A key sentence was "Last time I checked, no one in your neighborhood was planning an event. We need to make sure

---

[18] Saul Alinsky, *Rules for Radicals* (New York: Random House, 1971), 81.

> *that your neighbors have somewhere to gather and experience*
> *the President's big speech—and you could be that person."*

On Wednesday, August 29, Ruth went to the OFA office in Bellingham to talk with Colleen.

After a cordial OFA business discussion, Colleen asked Ruth, "Why don't you respect me?"

Ruth responded that she found it difficult to work with Colleen because she talked so rapidly that it was hard to follow. Colleen replied that Ruth wouldn't criticize her if she stuttered; that she knew she talked fast and was working on it. Colleen became emotional and said she needed to be by herself.

Ruth left, saying, "I'm sorry you're upset. I'll await word on the next steps."

That evening, Colleen sent a message proposing that Ruth meet with her and Amie the next day. Ruth agreed, and the meeting was set for one o'clock at a coffee shop near I-5 rather than at the OFA office. (Possibly because Colleen and Amie did not want to disturb others who might be working there.)

The first thing Amie said to Ruth was, "We don't want to lose you."

Ruth said she was there to resign. She had done her best and apparently that was not good enough. "Our team may have peaked too early. Maybe it's time to get a new team leader with fresh ideas, fresh approaches, and fresh relationships. I'm not walking out and slamming the door. I'll stay active and help with the transition."

Ruth thanked Amie for all she had done for us. They spoke briefly about logistics of the change and agreed to meet again after Labor Day. The next day, Ruth sent the following message:

> *Hello, team, Yesterday afternoon, I resigned as team leader of OFA's Whatcom Neighborhood Team. I will remain as an active volunteer. For information on planned activities, contact the core team coordinator of your area of interest. If the position is vacant, contact our field organizer, Colleen. See attached organization list in .doc for PCs and .pages for Macs. An interim [or] replacement team leader will be introduced soon. In the meantime, I urge you to continue doing the good work you have been doing for the reelection of President Obama and in the reelection or election of other key Democrats. It has been my pleasure to work with you, and I look forward to seeing you at upcoming events.*

Postscript

Miscommunication continued to plague the September 6 event. Colleen told the new fall fellow, who took over as the Whatcom team leader, that she had contacted the scheduled host to inform him of the consolidation of the Whatcom team with the Bellingham event.

However, about six o'clock that evening, the host called Ruth, asking, "What's going on? I've got two people here but nobody from OFA."

"Didn't you get a call telling you it was moving to Bellingham?" Ruth asked.

"No."

"I am so sorry. As you know, I'm no longer in charge, but you all could go to Bellingham."

However, Ruth did not know the site of the Bellingham event, and none of the people gathered there wanted to travel to Bellingham, so the host persuaded them to stay as his guests and watch the president. A fortunate decision because, shortly after, another volunteer arrived.

LESSONS LEARNED

Our experiences led us to the following conclusions:

- **Honor volunteers' interests.** A variety of tasks awaits OFA volunteer assignment. If some dislike phone calling, they may love inputting data. If others detest door-to-door canvassing, they may adore registering voters.

- **Treat volunteers as precious resources, not menial conscripts.** Ask. Don't tell. Explain the why, not just the what of your request. Seek suggestions on the how.

- **Utilize the varied backgrounds of volunteers—school superintendents, psychologists, instrumentation technicians, teachers, business owners, pastors, engineers, software consultants, musicians, chefs, and administrators may be on your team.** Their varied knowledge and talents richly contribute to all events.

- **Recognize that volunteers come with full lives.** Family responsibilities, civic duties, and personal recreation may take precedence over campaign plans.
- **Practice all the characteristics of good leadership.** Start with communication, and add empathy, honesty, fairness, and intelligence.
- **Remember that respect of volunteers begets respect of leaders.** What goes around comes around. Give what you expect to receive.

EPILOGUE

In the month following, we considered what we learned in leading our neighborhood team over the past year. While continuing to volunteer with OFA at the nonleadership level, we have supported other campaigns.

On the last Wednesday in September, Ruth and another local PCO organized a Tipple & Talk event for the two Democratic Washington legislative candidates who were running against regressive incumbents. The sponsors gained a calendar listing in the local weekly newspaper well in advance, sent e-mail messages to their lists, and posted flyers. The turnout was close to forty people, filling all of the chairs in the top floor of the Via Birch Bay Café and Bistro, with a few people standing.

A neighbor, whose name we didn't know, attended. The next day, we saw two campaign signs in her window.

One of the reasons for the good turnout was that both candidates are popular. Natalie McClendon was the chair of the Whatcom County Democratic Party and a local business owner. Matt Krogh is well known as one of the leaders of the anti-coal terminal movement. The pro-terminal campaign is well-financed and offering jobs. Anti-terminal people are arguing against pollution in multiple forms and for new industries with clean jobs. Matt works as the North Sound bay keeper at ReSources for a Sustainable Community, focusing on water quality.

When he filed for the legislative position at the last minute, he needed a campaign manager and chose a twenty-three-year-old intern, Sam. She was a forestry major at the University of Washington. With no political science courses, she never thought of working in a campaign. But as Sam said, "Matt and I are figuring it out."

Tall and relaxed, Sam inspires confidence. One evening at the start of a previous meet and greet, Sam received a call from Matt, who was on his way and wanted to know if Sam had brought something.

"Matt, I think of everything." Sam smiled.

Every few days, Sam sends out phone bank and canvassing schedules for weeks in advance. There's nothing frenetic. Organization is certain.

Sam reflects the confident and relaxed candidate that is Matt. Were the failings we experienced caused by a frenetic upline? We don't know. But we do believe that leaders who depend on volunteers should want to attract and nurture people like Sam.

As for ourselves, Ruth is the PCO of the new precinct in which we live. This precinct, with over a thousand registered voters, is one of the largest in the county. Working together, we intend to get to know as many of those voters as we can in this election. We started on this path in the 2008 campaign when we canvassed many of the homes as volunteers.

At the Tipple & Talk, Nat and Matt spoke mostly about education and jobs. They didn't talk about the coal terminal until one man, who didn't know much about Matt, asked where he stood on the issue. Matt answered that most of his day job now was devoted to opposing the terminal. Nat explained that, in addition to the Army Corps of Engineers, the most important decision body is the Whatcom County Council.

And she added, "The majority of the county council members are up for reelection next year. Anti-coal candidates are preparing to run."

We are likely to support them.

The last Friday in September, Ruth attended a Planned Parenthood fund-raising luncheon. While she was talking with Sandra Fluke, Philip A. Dwyer of the *Bellingham Herald* took a picture of an animated Fluke. That's part of Ruth on the right.

The last Sunday in October, with just ten days remaining before the election and ballots having been mailed to all Washington registered voters on the 19th, Ruth and her cohorts, working with the Whatcom Dems, held a repeat event at the Via Birch Bay Café and Bistro. They called it a Congressional Conversation, a meeting with Suzan DelBene, the 1st Congressional District candidate,

In our vacant lot fronting Birch Bay Drive, the main thoroughfare, we put up signs for Barack

Obama, Jay Inslee, Suzan DelBene, Natalie McClendon and Matt Krogh. We are extending our commitment down the ballot to the promise of Organizing for America.

ACKNOWLEDGEMENTS

We want to thank all the volunteers who contributed in large and small ways to our experience. Below, listed in alphabetical order, are many of the members of our neighborhood team. Apologies to anyone we failed to acknowledge.

Marit Aldrich
Jodee Arnold
Richard Arnold
Dalen Bayes
Lori Bayes
John H. Binns Jr.
Alice (Sunny) Brown
Jim Byrnes
Susan Carpenter
Karen Catlin
Grace Cisneros
Ben Craft

Donna Dietrich
Jamieson Dietrich
Bryan Dixon
Nini Dixon
Jenny Donatelli
Andi Douglass
Pat Elwell
Mel Finnson
Karen Flood
Meredith Ford
Lorren Garlichs
Gail Garman

Nan Geer
Brenda Graves
Don Griffiths
Linda Griffiths
Sandra Hansen
Bonnie Hathaway
Jerry Hathaway
Jan Hamilton
Kathryn Hanowell
George Holmes
Susan Holmes
Gretchen Hoyt
Howard Jachter
Sonja Jansen
Andrew Jones
Ken Jones
Kitty King
Janet Lutz-Smith
Shelly Madsen
Ana Rose Madsen
Gretchen McFarland
Tim McMurry
Joy Monjure
Stanley Monks
Naomi Murphy
Roger Murphy

Joan Parrish
Liana Parrish
Gregory Ptisch Jr.
David Polen
Ann Quiggle
Sandra Renner
April Schoenmakers
Suzanne Schwake
Mary Stack
Alexis Staley
Sandy Staley
Beth Standen
Jeremy Standen
Donna Starr
Jim Stewart
Peggy Stewart
Bob Storms
Margo Thorpe
Louisa Underwood
John Veleber
Bill Warner
Nancy Weisz
Nancy Wiebe
Alyce Werkema
Helen Worley

We also want to express our appreciation to all of the creative and resourceful people at iUniverse who produced this book in remarkable time. They include Dianne Lee, Jeff Hecita, Krista Hill, Jan Ley, and Jill Serinas.

ABOUT THE AUTHORS

Al Krause and Ruth Higgins have been together since 1992. She was living in Salt Lake City; he was living in San Francisco. They met in the home of friends in Seattle and married in the same house in 1994.

Ruth, who grew up near Vancouver, British Columbia, first worked in hospital medical records, then x-ray technology, and finally quality measurement and improvement. A graduate of Westminster College in Utah who earned an MBA at Fontbonne University in St. Louis, she held various management and education positions with the Veterans Administration, the University of Utah Medical Center, and Chinese Hospital in San Francisco.

Al, a graduate of Westminster College in Pennsylvania, served three years in the Army Security Agency, including a tour in Korea. He then worked ten years in advertising in Philadelphia and over thirty years in public relations in San Francisco, primarily in his own firms.

Old enough to collect Social Security but too young to retire, they moved to Birch Bay, Washington, in 2003, where they've been active in community affairs. Their writing has appeared in newspapers, magazines, two anthologies and their own blogs.

Al and Ruth have been somewhat active in politics for many years. Al handled communications for a State Senate campaign and assisted a Board of Supervisors candidate in

San Francisco. As a publicist, while the bulk of his work was in the investment community, he promoted studies by the Council on Economic Priorities, the Council on Municipal Performance and other public service non-profits.

Ruth volunteered on issue campaigns in Seattle and a congressional candidate's campaign in Salt Lake City. The divisive tactics of the Republican Party, along with the stalled Congress and the hateful rhetoric, propelled them into extreme activism in 2011.

Ruth joined OFA in July 2011. She and Al, working in phone banks, made something like twenty-five hundred calls. To those sessions in team members' homes, they estimate they took three hundred liters of Merlot and fifteen thousand grams of peanut butter pretzels.